FAIR NIGHTS . . . AND SUNNY DAYS

Pour Laurence

Pour toujours......
...... Aloha

Guy Buffet's

Hawaii

FAIR NIGHTS . . . AND SUNNY DAYS

with text by Ronn Ronck

Twenty-Six Original Paintings
reproduced for framing

Published by Cameron and Company
San Francisco, California

Acknowledgments

Special thanks and aloha for their friendship and assistance from Guy Buffet to:
Ron Adams, Michael Azevedo, François Benoist, Laurence Buffet, Nathan Ching, Kevin Baptist, Marcel Boussioux, Gerald Britt,
Simon Charbonnier, Lucien Charbonnier, David Clarke, Lou Campbell, Michel Cardon, Michele Counil, Dan Elliott,
Max Eyssallene, Les Enderton, Pierre Ernst, Charles Feeney, Susan Fletcher, Antoine Ernst, Jack Gardner, Darcel Gilbert,
Dick Hetfer, Cyril Ishard, William Johnston, Bernard Jacoupy, Father Keaki, Marty Khan, Bob Longhi, Carl Lindquist,
Gerard Lelievre, Maurice Lasnier, Michel Martin, John McCotter, David Milligan, Adi Kolher, Ron Munoz, Steve Miller,
Richard Nelson, Bernard Nogues, Jean Claude Perrin, Alan Pollock, Peter Radulovic, Mary Richard, Rick Reed, Alan Robin,
Gerard Reversade, Mark Shklor, Walter Strode, Ernest Scheerer, Gerald Sterns, Gary and Andrea Smith, Albert Stoltze,
Rob Thibaut, Mayor Hannibal Tavares, Patricia Vazonne, Alex Wilson, James Whitaker, John Wittenbury, Mladen Zorkin,
and of course my little Nicole.

CAMERON and COMPANY
543 Howard Street, San Francisco, California 94105

Library of Congress Catalogue number: 87-071222
Guy Buffet's Hawaii Fair Nights and Sunny Days ISBN 0-918684-31-5
©1987 by Robert W. Cameron and Company, Inc. All rights reserved.
Paintings and illustrations ©1987 by Guy Buffet
Text ©1987 by Ronn Ronck

First Printing, 1987

Book design by
JANE OLAUG KRISTIANSEN

Typography by Parker-Smith Typography, San Francisco.
Color Separations and Printing by Dai Nippon Printing Co., Tokyo, Japan.

SPECIAL THANKS
to Robert Cameron,
my dear publisher, better
known as "Uncle Bob,"
and my friend
Todd Cameron.

SPECIAL ALOHA
to my art dealer
and "big" brother,
Jim Killett.

PRIMITIVE ARTIST
IN AN IMPRESSIONISTIC SETTING

Artists sometimes take themselves too seriously. They present themselves to the public as mysterious figures who hide away in their studios waiting for the right inspiration to hit. When it finally comes they are able to produce one masterpiece after another in strong bursts of creative energy.

"There may be a few great artists around who operate this way," Buffet admits, "but for most of us this kind of image is nothing more than a romantic dream. Inspiration seldom pops out of the sky. Artists are successful because of good training, hard work, and quite a bit of luck."

Look at Buffet's painting on the following page. *L'artiste est fatigué,* the artist is tired. After drinking several glasses of a favorite red wine, he has put down his brushes for awhile and is taking a nap with his dog.

Buffet has grown a beard for this self-portrait but he can't disguise the paintings on the wall. While they may differ in style, they are obviously all from the hand of the same sleepy French artist.

"I've never been too concerned about the way I paint," Buffet states, "because I've never consciously tried to develop a style. Sometimes I feel like being a primitive or naïve painter, at other times I feel more like being an impressionist. I think the only thing I don't like to be is abstract."

Buffet is a very articulate artist but he has no idea why the people in his paintings do what they do. He has no idea, for example, why the artist in this painting has put a nude Canadian woman on a pink horse.

The little dog doesn't know the answer to that interesting question either. He just stares at the viewer as if to say, "please leave the artist alone for awhile. He's waiting around for some more inspiration to strike."

GUY BUFFET AND HIS ART
by Ronn Ronck

Several years ago I was watching Guy Buffet paint a mural that wrapped around two outer walls of the Waimanalo Community-School Library. A number of young students had also gathered to watch and were taking a strong interest in the artist at work.

One third-grader, her arms full of library books, looked at the mural for a while and then turned to Buffet with a direct question. "Mister," she asked, "do you get paid for doing this?"

After a few seconds of stunned silence, Buffet started to laugh. "Well," he said, answering the girl, "let me put it this way. I'd probably still do it even if I didn't get paid."

Buffet returned to his painting but a smile seemed to linger on his face for the rest of the morning. Later he told me that, when he was a youngster growing up in Paris, it never occurred to him to ask such questions.

"Art had little connection to money in those days," he explained. "I became a painter primarily for the pleasure it gave myself and others."

Rising in the distance behind Waimanalo School are the Koolau Mountains. Dominating this side of Oahu, they appear to change colors according to the time of day and weather. Their chiseled summits float in and out of the rain-sopped mist.

After Buffet was commissioned to do the mural, he took a series of walks in the area to "capture the feeling of Waimanalo." His eyes returned so often to the Koolaus that he finally decided to make them a primary reference point in his mural, a 60-foot-long work of art that he titled "Waimanalo Love Song."

"The mural uses the mountains and ocean as a backdrop," Buffet told me at the time, "but I really wanted to celebrate the influence of Hawaiian music in the everyday life of the people here. Individual scenes show people having a backyard party, a guy playing his guitar at the beach, and a country band."

Buffet's beautiful mural, dedicated in April 1980, has become something of a tourist attraction. For those who can't make the visit to Waimanalo, however, four of the preliminary paintings: "Talk story," "Surfer Watching Waves," "Hawaiian Love Song," and "Gabby," are reproduced in the first volume of *Guy Buffet's Hawaii*. Elements of each were incorporated into the finished mural.

The spirit of Waimanalo has also been carried over into this present book. Its title, *Fair Nights and Sunny Days*, refers to the two paintings partly shown on the front and back covers, and completely reproduced in this book. They were done soon after the mural was completed, as evidenced by their full titles, "Fair Nights in Waimanalo" and "Sunny Days in Waimanalo."

"People living in Hawaii," Buffet says, "will recognize a special meaning behind the title. Our weather is always so nice here that local forecasters have come up with a stock phrase to describe it. They never stop telling us that we can look forward to 'fair nights and sunny days' and, most of the time, they're right."

Guy Buffet was born in Paris on January 13, 1943. His parents, although in the restaurant business, were fond of art and he learned early that his neighborhood had once nourished the budding talents of Chagall, Matisse, Picasso, and Modigliani. "There was plenty of talk about these famous painters at home," he says, "and I used to listen to these conversations while I did my homework at the kitchen table. I remember beginning to draw on napkins and the linen tablecloths."

On his 12th birthday his mother gave him his first box of paints, a couple of brushes, a wooden easel, and plenty of canvases. The young Buffet was soon displaying his paintings on the walls of the family restaurant. His first sale, at the age of 13, was to a visiting American eager to take a charming souvenir of Paris back home.

When he was 14 he enrolled in the Beaux Arts de Toulon and from there went to study advanced art and design at the Academie de Peinture de la Ville de Paris. During the evenings he worked in the restaurant as a busboy.

"My first commission," Buffet remembers, "came from the chef. He had bought a cheap paintings of a winter scene in a furniture store and, after a year or so, got tired of looking at it. He paid me to change the scene into spring by painting over the bare trees and snow. It was always a great joke between us."

At the age of 18 he was called into the French Navy and sailed around the world aboard the cruiser *De Grasse*. He began as a regular deckhand but soon convinced the captain that the ship needed an artist to document the voyage. His humorous drawings and watercolors delighted the officers and crew.

Every French artist is familiar with the story of Paul Gauguin and his sojourn in Tahiti. Buffet got his first chance to see this legendary paradise in 1962 when the *De Grasse* sailed into the South Pacific and anchored in the harbor at Papeete.

"While I was on shore leave with some fellow sailors," Buffet says, "we were picked up hitchhiking by a motorist who identified himself as the mayor of the city. After visiting the ship and seeing some of my paintings he talked to the captain and got permission for me to put on an exhibit in town."

What Buffet needed most, however, were some scenes of Tahiti. He spent the next three weeks, while the *De Grasse* took a side trip through the Tuamotu Islands, painting as fast as he could. In June 1962 he had his first one-man show at the Gallerie Mourareau in Papeete. The exhibit consisted of about 50 watercolors. It was a complete sellout.

Buffet had a second one-man show during the ship's visit to Noumea, New Caledonia, and then, upon his return to France, at the Museum of the French Navy in Toulon. An influential admiral saw the latter show and arranged for Buffet to be designated an "official" French military artist.

At his request he was reassigned to the *Jeanne d'Arc*, another cruiser on its way to the Pacific. In 1963 the ship docked in Honolulu and Buffet was asked to exhibit his paintings at the Royal Hawaiian Art Gallery which is still located in the Royal Hawaiian Hotel in Waikiki.

While preparing for the exhibit Buffet was introduced to members of the prominent Cooke family. Hawaii's major art museum, the Honolulu Academy of Arts, had been founded by the late Mrs. Charles M. (Anna) Cooke and opened its doors in 1927. The Cooke family invited him to return to Hawaii after his Navy discharge and offered to provide living and studio space.

Buffet accepted the invitation and returned to the Islands in 1964. He spent a year in Honolulu, working under the Cooke's patronage. In 1965, when the urge to move came again, Buffet headed for California. He settled in San Francisco and remained there for eight years.

It was perfect timing. San Francisco was then the focus of a cultural revolution that made the Haight-Ashbury district famous overnight. During the "Summer of Love" in 1967 the streets were crowded with long-haired "hippies" who flooded into the city wearing beads around their necks and flowers in their hair. Psychedelic music, drugs, and new religious cults were free for the taking.

"Lots of interesting things were happening in San Francisco during these days," Bufet says, "and it was a great place to be. I found abundant subject matter for my paintings.

"On the negative side I had to continually hustle for commissions in California and did a number of money-making projects that I didn't enjoy. Once I even was asked to paint bright flowers and smiling faces on the walls of a funeral home chapel."

Buffet returned to Honolulu in 1973. His stay in San Francisco had included annual trips to Hawaii and during each visit he felt revitalized by the climate, beauty, and lifestyle of the islands.

Galleries and collectors had also proven responsive to his painting.

One of his biggest fans was Robert B. Goodman, a former photographer for *National Geographic* and *Life* magazines. While Buffet was living in San Francisco, he had started Island Heritage, a publishing company devoted to books about Hawaii. Goodman had kept in touch and now asked Buffet to illustrate a half-dozen children's picture books based on Hawaiian folklore. The Island Heritage series was quite successful and all of the books, published during the early 1970s, remain in print.

In 1975 the Hawaii State Foundation on Culture and the Arts commissioned Buffet to create a series of 12 paintings under the general theme of "Hawaii's Forgotten People and Places." These paintings, accompanied by descriptions from local journalist, Leonard Lueras, became an exhibit that travelled throughout the state. The State Foundation on Culture and the Arts also commissioned the Waimanalo mural from Buffet and an earlier one he painted at the Kaimuki Library in Honolulu.

Buffet's introduction to Maui came in 1977 when he was asked by Maui gallery-owner Helen Byron to produce 100 watercolors depicting scenes on the Valley Island. Some of these were subsequently published in two print portfolios under the title of "Maui, An Intimate Look." In 1979 he spent several months in French Polynesia, painting

there for the first time since his days in the Navy. The following year Buffet was given a one-man-show at the Gallerie Vaite in Papeete, Tahiti.

Another close friend in Hawaii is Michel Martin, the founder of Chez Michel, a garden-style French restaurant in Honolulu. Buffett decorated the restaurant with his paintings and together they published several illustrated portfolios of French recipes. He has also done a number of paintings documenting Martin's career in France, San Francisco, and Hawaii.

Buffet's first limited edition serigraph, "Cows on Roller Skates," was released in 1980. Many others have followed. Buffet's paintings and graphics are represented by his friend, Jim Killett, who owns the Lahaina Galleries group (including the Kapalua Gallery) on Maui. Later in 1980 noted San Francisco aerial photographer/publisher Robert Cameron published the first volume of *Guy Buffet's Hawaii*. Cameron, who has also published *Fair Nights and Sunny Days*, is well-known for his book, *Above Hawaii*, and other *Above* aerial portraits of San Francisco, Los Angeles, Yosemite, Washington, New York, London, and Paris. Cameron and Company also publishes an annual *Guy Buffet's Hawaii* wall calendar and note cards.

At the end of 1980 Buffet visited China as a guest of the Peking Arts and Crafts Council, the official state agency which supplies goods to stores inside and out-

side the country. That trip included tours of Canton, Hangchow, Shanghai, Tientsin, and Peking. Buffet completed 40 watercolors on the trip and numerous pen-and-ink drawings which have been widely exhibited. He is looking forward to another visit to China and plans to publish a separate book on that country.

The year 1983 was another turning point in Buffet's career. During the summer he returned to Paris for his first extended visit to France since moving to Hawaii. Twenty years later he rediscovered his French heritage and also found a Parisian wife, Laurence, whom he married in 1984. In January 1986 he was given his first one-man show in Paris at La Coupole, a historic cafe in Montparnasse that has been frequented by generations of French artists and writers. The exhibit was co-sponsored by Jim Killett and one of Buffet's major clients, the French champagne house of Perrier-Jouet.

Today, Guy and Laurence divide their time between Maui, where they have a townhouse in Kapalua, and France, where they have an apartment in Paris. In between, Buffet's painting trips and exhibit openings take them on frequent trips around the world.

ARTISTS BY THE ZOO FENCE

There were only a handful of art galleries in Honolulu when Buffet first visited here in 1963 as a French Navy artist. While his ship, *Jeanne de Arc*, was in port he had a one-man show of his watercolor paintings in the Royal Hawaiian (Hotel) Art Gallery.

A year later, returning to Honolulu after his discharge, Buffet continued to show his paintings around the state. In addition to regular gallery shows he sometimes exhibited his work on the Zoo Fence.

Buffet is only one of many noted artists in Hawaii who have sold their works on this fence, located on the outside of the Honolulu Zoo and across from Kapiolani Park. Local artists take their paintings to the fence every Saturday and Sunday and display them for local residents and tourists who are staying in Waikiki.

Since there is no overhead — and the artists deal directly with the buyers — prices on the fence are lower than can be found elsewhere. Collectors also dream about discovering a talented new artist before fame arrives.

The Zoo Fence hasn't changed much in the past two decades and Buffet stops by whenever he visits the Waikiki area. A few of his friends still exhibit their paintings here and the talk brings back fond memories of his early days in Honolulu.

One fanciful ingredient included in this painting are the animals looking over the top of the fence. Buffet frequently uses animals in his paintings and their humorous expressions have always delighted his fans.

"While doing this watercolor scene," Buffet says, "I had the urge to take my painting off the easel and put it up on the fence alongside all the rest of the works. But then I wondered if anybody would buy it. Perhaps that baldheaded tourist with the glasses, or the lady with the bikini panties, are looking for more serious paintings. The elephant, though, seems to understand."

Collection: Ingrid Barnes

SHAVED ICE ON ALOHA FRIDAY

The women in this painting are wearing muu muus, the loose comfortable dress that has been a favorite of island women since the early days of the Christian missionaries. According to historical accounts the missionary wives designed this gown to gracefully accommodate the full figures of the Hawaiian women.

"Women often wear muu muus in my paintings," Buffet says, "because I love their beautiful printed patterns and bright colors. I don't use models, however, and none of these muu muus really exist outside of my imagination. Perhaps someday a fashion company will ask me to design my own line of muu muus."

Every Friday is Aloha Friday in Hawaii. The popular custom began in 1965 when the Hawaiian Fashion Guild asked residents to wear their colorful aloha shirts and muu muus on the last day of each work week. When local airlines and other corporations pledged their support of the plan "Aloha Friday" was officially decreed by the members of Honolulu's city council.

"Friday is my favorite day of the week in Hawaii," Buffet says, "because it is the most colorful. In addition to their pretty print dresses the women also wear flowers in their hair, and sparkles in their eyes."

During lunch time on a recent Aloha Friday these four island women were sitting in a park and talking story. Buffet says they must have just come from a snack bar since they were eating shaved ice (or "shave ice"), a local treat of ice flakes covered with various flavors of sweet syrup. On the Mainland a smaller version of this popular snack is called a snowcone.

"I have no idea what they were gossiping about," Buffet says. "Maybe they didn't like that Frenchman in the funny aloha shirt who kept staring at them from across the street."

Collection: Stan Sax

WAIPIO VALLEY

When the ancient Polynesians first arrived on the Big Island they found a large horseshoe-shaped valley chiseled out of the windy northern coast. They called this natural fortress Waipio, the land of the "Curved Water."

The name probably came from the curving shoreline and black sand beach located at the mile-wide opening of the valley. The other three sides, tapering back six miles, are protected by up to 3,000-foot cliffs.

At one time, according to oral tradition, about 40,000 people lived in Waipio Valley. They tended small farm plots and fished in the fresh water river that ran the length of the lush valley.

"This was an extremely tight-knit community," Buffet explains, "a fact that had much to do with Waipio's isolation from the rest of the Big Island. The only way in or out of the valley was by sea during calm weather or by narrow footpaths that wound up the steep cliffs. I wouldn't doubt that some people spent their whole lives in Waipio without ever seeing the outside world."

By the time of European discovery the population of Waipio had probably shrunk to less than 5,000. When the missionary William Ellis visited the valley in 1823 he counted 1,325 residents in several small villages aong the cliff sides.

At the start of World War II there were less than 200 inhabitants in a tidy village that included a few stores, a church, a post office, and even a little red one-room school house. Disaster hit in 1946, however, when a massive tidal wave sent a 55-foot-high column of water pounding through the valley.

"Less than two dozen people live in Waipio now," Buffet says. "On a hike into the valley a few years ago I found this small farmhouse hidden among the trees. It was as peaceful a spot as I've ever found in Hawaii."

Private Collection

BELLOWS BEACH

There is more to Hawaii than beaches but it's difficult to convince visitors that the Islands also have other attractions. Hawaii will probably never outgrow its romantic image of sun, sand, and sea.

Beaches, of course, are loved by local people as well. The early Polynesian voyagers were tied to the water and they built their villages close to the beaches. Here on the warm sand they built their canoes and mended their fishing nets. For relaxation they often took their hand-carved surfboards into the water to see who could ride the biggest waves.

Today going to the beach is still a very important part of the island lifestyle. During the week, when people are working for a living, every sunny day is described as "a good day for the beach."

Hawaii's beaches, except for the tourist spots in Waikiki, are fairly deserted on weekdays. On weekends, however, the more popular beaches can get fairly crowded. Sometimes it seems like everyone in the state is out to catch a suntan, enjoy a picnic lunch, and watch the girls stroll by in their tiny bikinis.

In this inviting painting Buffet has pictured Bellows, a popular local beach in Waimanalo, Oahu. Bellows Field Beach Park, open to the public on weekends, is part of Bellows Air Force Base.

Bellows, due to its protection by the military, is relatively undeveloped and the area behind the wide beach has plenty of trees to shield picnickers from the tropic sun. The shallow waters and gentle shorebreak are perfect for beginning surfers.

"One day I was painting at home in my studio," Buffet explains, "and I was having a lot of trouble doing another scene. It was a beautiful day and I asked my wife if she wanted to go to the beach. She said I didn't have time to mess around. I went back into the studio and imagined what I'd missed by painting this view of Bellows."

Private Collection

KIMO'S

The old whaling port of Lahaina has been witness to a fascinating history. It was the first capital of the Hawaiian Kingdom and, during the mid-1800s, became the most famous port of the Pacific whaling fleet. Hundreds of ships called here each year from the 1820s through the 1860s.

Front Street in Lahaina has changed relatively little in appearance during the last century. Some of its buildings actually remain from the whaling days while others are more recent additions that were designed to appear like the originals.

Kimo's restaurant is located in one of these historic-looking buildings. Its simple design, weathered wood, and shuttered windows, take customers back to the 19th century. The restaurant's popular second-story balcony would have delighted a sea captain used to walking the bridge.

This painting was commissioned by the three owners of Kimo's: Rob Thibaut, Sandy Saxten, and Dicky Moon. It was also reproduced by the restaurant for a promotional poster and a limited edition lithograph. Kimo's is one of several Hawaii restaurants that have featured Buffet's art in various ways. Others are Chez Michel and Bon Appetit on Oahu and Longhi's, Chez Paul, Gerard's, and the Grill and Bar on Maui.

"Lahaina residents and frequent visitors," Buffet says, "will recognize many of the people I've included in this painting. Besides the restaurant's owners and employees, there are a few local characters that are always hanging around town."

Since moving permanently to Maui in 1982, Buffet has painted many scenes of Lahaina. "I came to Hawaii as a French sailor-artist," he explains, "and I still have a little bit of the sea in my blood. Sometimes I wish that I could have jumped ship here in the 1820s. I wonder what my paintings would have been like had I been around during the great whaling days?"

Collection: Rob Thibaut and Sandy Saxten

BABY PIGS CROSSING

Hana, on the southeastern end of Maui, is one of Hawaii's most isolated communities. To get here drivers must first navigate a slow and narrow 50-mile road that winds its way along a scenic cliff-lined coast. Hundreds of curves and several dozen one-lane bridges add to the experience.

For over a century Hana was known as a sugar plantation town. Then after World War II the sugar business died and Hana Ranch was formed. Its 4,500 acres now support a herd of 9,000 white-faced Hereford cattle. Cattle, in fact, outnumber the residents of Hana almost ten to one.

Buffet has visited "Heavenly Hana" many times, even more so since his good friend, Carl Lindquist, has become manager of the Hotel Hana-Maui. During one of his trips Buffet came across a small handmade wooden sign nailed to a roadside tree that said "Caution. Baby Pigs Crossing."

No pigs were in sight but Buffet stopped his car anyway and parked alongside the road. He started making the sketches that eventually became this painting. Twenty minutes later he heard a rustling in the woods and three little pigs scampered by in front of him.

"While doing this painting back in my studio," Buffet says, "I began to think about Hana some more. Any place that would put up a sign like this to protect its pigs would be a great place to live. With just a little bit of envy I decided to put my own name on the mailbox."

Art critics, as a rule, don't like "cute" paintings. Buffet doesn't care. He paints to please himself first; then his audience. The critics never even enter his mind.

"The truth of the matter," Buffet explains, "is that a lot of people like cute things but don't want to get caught admitting it. These little piggies don't care either way. All they want to do is get across the road."

Private Collection

WAHINE BY THE SEA

Women have long been the favorite subject matter of Hawaii's artists, male or female. Exotic island *wahines* have captivated the eye and the palette since the earliest image of a hula girl playing her ukulele on the beach under a swaying palm tree.

In more recent times the depiction of Hawaiian women gained wide attention through the paintings of Madge Tennent (1889-1972). Born in England, Tennent was raised in South Africa and there showed an early talent for art. She was sent to Paris where she took classes at the Academie Julian.

Tennent returned to South Africa after her studies, married a successful accountant, and followed her husband to Hawaii where they made their home.

Here she began to paint the women of the Islands, eventually turning them into heroic figures, large of body yet graceful and elegant. She applied her paint to the canvas with a knife instead of a brush, plastering it on in a swirl of bright colors.

"Unfortunately," Buffet says with regret, "I never met Madge Tennent. By the time I arrived in Hawaii she was in her 70s and retired from painting. But I got to know her work by visiting the Tennent Gallery which she established in Honolulu. She taught me not only about the rhythm of shape and color but also about the special dignity that comes so naturally to Hawaiian women."

Over the years Buffet has painted hundreds of women, but this portrait of a young lady, relaxing in her house by the sea is a favorite. The title of this work is now "Wahine By The Sea" but at one point it was called "Intimate Relationship," a reference to the cute little puppy which sits on the woman's lap.

"While I was doing this painting I thought I knew what this young woman was thinking," Buffet says. "Today I'm not so sure. She is quiet, beautiful, and a little mysterious. Only her dog knows what secrets may hide behind those dark glowing eyes and soft smile."

Private Collection

ROYAL HAWAIIAN HOTEL

The Royal Hawaiian Hotel, sometimes called the "Pink Palace of the Pacific," is the most famous hotel in Waikiki. It sits on a 16-acre site that was once used as a summer home for Hawaii's kings and queens.

Built to accommodate the growing number of tourists arriving in the Islands, the six-story beach-front hotel was opened in 1927. Its architectural influence can be traced to the romantic movies of the period, particularly to the Spanish-Moorish sets used in the shooting of Rudolph Valentino's classic film, *The Sheik*.

"Nobody is quite sure," Buffet says, "why the hotel was first painted pink. Soft pastel colors, though, are quite common in the tropics. Pink reminds me of a rosy island sunset."

During the late 1920s and 1930s the Royal Hawaiian Hotel was a glamorous playground for travelers arriving by luxury passenger liner. Douglas Fairbanks and Mary Pickford frequented the Royal as did Clark Gable and Cary Grant. Bing Crosby's 1938 movie, *Waikiki Wedding*, used the hotel as its backdrop.

After the Japanese attacked Pearl Harbor on Dec. 7, 1941, the Royal was closed to tourists and taken over by the government. The military forces used its facilities throughout World War II as a rest and relaxation center for sailors, soldiers, and marines serving in the Pacific.

"This painting," Buffet explains, "is my idea of how the hotel might have looked during the war years. Every sailor's dream was to spend a week at the Royal with a pretty island girl all his own."

Buffet, himself, first saw the hotel while in uniform. He was an official French Navy artist when his ship visited Honolulu in 1962. A year later he returned for his first art exhibit in Hawaii, an exhibit held in the Royal Hawaiian Hotel Gallery.

Private Collection

RIDING TO THE MAKAWAO RODEO

Makawao is a quiet cowboy town in eastern Maui. It sits surrounded by picturesque ranch lands that stretch up the western flank of Haleakala, the inactive volcano that dominates this side of the island.

The earliest inhabitants of Makawao were Portuguese laborers who settled here in the late 1800s. After their contracts with the sugar plantations ran out they took their hard-earned money and built a new life centered around horses and cattle.

Life in Makawao retained its rural character until World War II when the U.S. Marines stationed troops in the nearby village of Kokomo. Dozens of small stores sprang up along main street in Makawao to provide services for the military.

When the war ended, the Marines left, and most of these businesses closed their doors. Makawao's *paniolos*, the Hawaiian word for cowboys, climbed into their saddles and rode back onto the range.

"During the past few years," Buffet says, "changes have come again to Makawao. A new prosperity has reopened many of the old stores that have stood vacant for decades. There are lots of new homes being built in the area and visitors find the place a charming detour on the way to Haleakala."

In this painting Buffet shows a line of riders on their way to the famous Makawao Rodeo which is held every Fourth of July weekend in an arena outside of town. The annual event, begun in 1955, is the largest rodeo in Hawaii and features the best competitors from throughout the state.

"Makawao is the only true *paniolo* town left in Maui," Buffet says, "and everybody from miles around puts on their hats and boots and rides to the rodeo. The competitors are serious but there's also plenty of fun. This is probably the most exciting three-day party in Hawaii."

Private Collection

STEAMER DAYS

During the first half of this century, before the age of airplanes, the arrival of a passenger liner in downtown Honolulu called for a gala celebration. Bands played, hula girls danced, and colorful streamers were thrown down from the upper deck of the ship.

"Today it only takes a few hours to fly here from the Mainland," Buffet says, "but in those days it took over a week to get here by steamer. The ships carried not only people but cargo and mail as well."

Steamer Days – sometimes called Boat Days – were irregular at first due to the arrivals and departures of nearly a dozen different lines. Then, in 1910, Matson Navigation Company entered the profitable San Francisco to Honolulu run and its

ships became the main link between the Mainland and Hawaii.

For many years the sleek Matson Navigation Company ships arrived in Honolulu every Tuesday morning. Tuesday thus became known as Steamer Day.

Construction of the Aloha Tower, shown in the background of this painting, began in late 1924 and was completed in 1926. The 184-foot waterfront skyscraper, with its seven-ton clock soon became the centerpiece of Steamer Days activities.

The grandest of all Steamer Days probably occurred in 1927 with the maiden voyage arrival of the *Malolo*, a 582-foot Matson superliner that carried 650 first-class passengers and whose luxurious accommodations were unmatched by any other

ship afloat. Cruising at 21-knots the *Malolo* ("flying fish") was able to make the trip from San Francisco in only four and a half days.

"The heyday of the old steamers," Buffet explains, "ended with the Great Depression and the 1935 flight of the Pan American Clipper which opened up the Islands to air travel. During World War II the Matson ships were confiscated by the U.S. Navy and put into use as troop carriers."

Private Collection

HULIHEE PALACE

Hulihee Palace sits on the shore of Kailua Bay on the Big Island, across from Mokuaikaua Church. it was built in 1838 as a summer residence for Hawaii's royalty and it served as their vacation retreat until 1916.

Mokuaikaua Church, just behind the palace in this painting, is composed of black lava rock walls joined by white coral mortar. Completed a year earlier than the palace it is the oldest church still being used in the Islands.

The modest two-story palace was constructed like the church, with thick coral-mortared walls that were covered over with stucco. A second-floor lanai runs along the oceanfront side of the palace, trimmed with Victorian-style wooden railings.

"Hulihee Palace is one of the most beautiful small buildings in Hawaii," Buffet says. "I especially like to drive by and view it on a starry night from across the bay."

For nearly a century Hulihee Palace sheltered a succession of royal family owners, including King Kamehameha IV, Princess Bernice Bishop, King Kalakaua and Prince Kalanianaole. It was sold in 1914 but stood empty for years and slowly fell into disrepair.

In 1927 the property was brought by the Territorial government and turned over to the Daughters of Hawaii. This historical preservation organization is made up of women whose ancestors were in Hawaii before 1880.

The Daughters of Hawaii now operate Hulihee Palace as a museum. They have restored the building to the way it looked during the reign of King Kalakaua (1874-1891) and have located much of the original furnishings.

"Anyone who visits Hulihee Palace today," Buffet says, "can see the remarkable job done by the Daughters of Hawaii in preserving this important historic building. In this painting I have included a group of these women enjoying themselves at a party near the seawall."

Private Collection

RACES AT KAPIOLANI PARK

Kapiolani Park was dedicated by King Kalakaua in 1877 to honor his wife, Queen Kapiolani. Located near Diamond Head in Waikiki, it was the first public park in the Hawaiian Kingdom.

The most popular spectator sport at the time was horse racing and an oval track was built in the park for weekend events. Race day was a gala affair with hundreds of colorfully-dressed fans leaning against the fence and packing the grandstands.

During the mid-1970s, Buffet had a studio within walking distance of Kapiolani Park, on the third floor above Mac's Market. It was here that he and journalist Leonard Lueras collaborated on a two-year project titled "Forgotten People and Places of Hawaii" for the State Foundation on Culture and the Arts.

For this project Buffet did a series of 12 oil and acryllic paintings of little known incidents in Hawaii's history and Lueras contributed a short written description on each. Included was a painting of the race track at Kapiolani Park. All of the paintings now hang in public buildings around the state.

"Leonard is a very good writer," Buffet says, "and he is especially good with titles. He was so successful in naming this project, for example, that nobody remembers it anymore. I've almost forgotten it myself."

Such was the strange case of the painting on the opposite page. Buffet worked on it for about three months in 1983 with a growing sense of *deja vu.* Not until it was completed did he realize that he had already done a painting of the Kapiolani Park race track for the State Foundation project he did with Lueras eight years earlier.

"Today I can't recall what the earlier painting actually looks like. I don't even know where it's located. Perhaps it will be rediscovered one day by another writer for a project titled 'Forgotten Paintings and Stories of Hawaii.'"

Collection: Mr. and Mrs. Weir Stewart

MICHEL AND HIS TOMATOES

This painting was originally done for a book that remains unpublished. It depicts well-known Honolulu restauranteur Michel Martin in a garden of smiling tomatoes.

Martin, a Frenchman born in Nice, originally came to Hawaii in 1939 to take a job in the dining room of the Royal Hawaiian Hotel. During World War II he was recruited to cook for the Army and, afterwards, opened up a French restaurant in Wahiawa called Chez Michel, "The House of Michel."

This was the first of his four Oahu restaurants. In 1961 he opened Michel's at the Colony Surf, then left in 1972 to launch a second Chez Michel on Kalakaua Avenue in Waikiki. In 1980 he moved again and opened the present Chez Michel in Eaton Square.

Buffet met Martin shortly after the Kalakaua Avenue restaurant opened and a close friendship developed. Martin soon had the walls of Chez Michel covered with paintings by Buffet. Together thay published a series of illustrated French recipes and occasionally Martin even cleared away the tables in the restaurant to host receptions for Buffet's art exhibits.

A few years ago Buffet decided to honor Martin's career in Hawaii and did a series of paintings to be included, along with a text I had written, in a small commemorative book. This project never found a publisher but the paintings have been widely exhibited.

Martin prides himself on serving fresh vegetables in his restaurants and in this painting Buffet shows him in the garden at his farm. There is another meaning, though, behind these tomatoes. Martin refers to women as "tomatoes" and they are a constant amusement in his life.

Happy cows are a constant amusement in Buffet's life. Of course, like his friend, Michel Martin, he loves his tomatoes, too.

Private Collection

PINEAPPLE HARVESTING IN KAPALUA

Nobody really knows when the first pineapple was planted in the Hawaiian Islands. Some historians believe that the fruit, a native of South America, was first brought to these shores by early Spanish explorers who may have predated the 1778 discovery of Captain James Cook. Others think they arrived in the ships of later traders.

The first written record of island pineapple is an 1813 diary entry by a Spaniard named Don Francisco de Paula y Marin. He mentions planting wild pineapple in the Kona District of the Big Island.

Several different varieties of pineapples were planted in the years that followed and tests eventually showed that the Smooth Cayenne, originally imported from Jamaica, was the best suited to Hawaii's soil and climate.

In 1892 the first pineapple cannery was started in Honolulu to process the expanding crop. James D. Dole, the most famous name in local pineapple history, built his own Honolulu cannery in 1906 and helped to make pineapple the most recognizable symbol of Hawaii.

The Maui Pineapple Company was founded in 1832 and subsequently planted thousands of acres of pineapple between the sea and the West Maui Mountains. In the 1970s the company rolled back a small fraction of its pineapple acreage and built the Kapalua Resort hotel and condominium complex.

Buffet moved from Honolulu in 1982 and now lives at Kapalua. In this painting Buffet has imagined what the resort area might have looked like back in the early years of this century when the pineapple industry was in full swing.

"While I was painting this scene," Buffet says, "I thought about all the changes that have taken place in this spot. This is a rather romantic view of the hard life shared by those pineapple workers who once labored in the fields where my condominium now stands."

Collection: William Dietrich

KAPIOLANI PARK

Sometimes the idea or the subject matter for a painting just pops up unexpectedly. Buffet feels blessed when such occasions occur and has learned to take advantage of these inspirations in his work.

One recent morning he was taking a shortcut through Kapiolani Park when he came across the women depicted in the opposite painting. Although he was in a hurry he took out a piece of paper and did a quick sketch of the scene. He noted down the basic composition, the design of the tree roots, and the warm blanket of long grass.

"I couldn't tell if these women were related to each other or not," Buffet says, "but they were certainly good friends. For a moment I thought of stopping to say hello but then walked on past. They were probably happy to get away from all the men in their lives and didn't need another one to mess things up."

This painting falls into a long tradition that Buffet calls the "School of the Pacific." Paul Gauguin is the most famous graduate of this school but many others came before him or followed in his footsteps. Whether they painted in Tahiti, Samoa, Australia, or Hawaii, their collective work reflects the soft light, bright colors, and lush tropical landscapes of the islands. And, of course, the sensual brown-skinned women of the Pacific have long fascinated visiting artists.

Modern critics usually don't like paintings like this. They equate seriousness in art with an intellectual message and feel uncomfortable with paintings that don't have something to say. Art is not really art if it is simply beautiful to look at.

"Critics also distrust an artist who is too popular," Buffet says. "The public's response to a work of art means nothing to them. I don't agree. My walls at home are covered with paintings I enjoy looking at and living with. The critics can keep all the messages for themselves."

Private Collection

ALOHA LAHAINA

During 1846, the peak year for Lahaina's historic whaling trade, a recorded 429 ships stopped here to take on barrels of fresh water, food, and other supplies. The popular seaport town also offered recreation for the sailors in the form of gambling houses, cheap liquor, and willing women.

Today, the harbor at Lahaina is still one of the busiest anchorages in the state. Yachts from all over the world stop here regularly on their way between the U.S. Mainland, Asia, and the other islands in the Pacific.

Behind the yachts in this painting is a two-story green building with a reddish roof. This is the Pioneer Inn, a plantation-style structure that was opened as a hotel in 1901. It does not look any different now than in the old days and has been featured in several Hollywood movies.

"In recent years," Buffet says, "Lahaina has become a mecca for artists just as much as for sailors. There are now over a dozen galleries in town, each displaying the work of established artists right alongside those who are relatively unknown."

Buffet's paintings and prints can be found in Lahaina Galleries which is headquartered a few blocks away from the Pioneer Inn on Front Street. Gallery owner Jim Killett has become a Lahaina success story.

"Killett is an ex-football coach," Buffet explains, "who moved to Lahaina in 1976. He and his wife had some money saved up and they decided to buy a business. It was a pick between an ice cream parlor and an art gallery.

"He actually decided to buy the ice cream parlor but the owner neglected to tell his wife that he was interested in selling. When she finally found out about the deal she broke it off. Killett then turned around and purchased the art gallery."

That fateful choice made Killett a prominent man in the Hawaii art world. He now has four art galleries on Maui and another on the Big Island. They bring in millions of dollars and much of this involves Guy Buffet's paintings and prints.

"Lahaina," Buffet says, "is a very slow-paced town. Visitors have time to check out the galleries and appreciate the art. It is a great place for both the artists and their collectors."

Collection: Dr. and Mrs. Burns

CHRISTMAS EVE AT THE MENEHUNES

On his bookshelves at home Buffet has a large collection of picture books for children. Some are in French, others in English. A few, picked up on his travels, are in languages that he does not even understand. All have one thing in common: the beauty or charm of their illustrations.

"When I was a youngster growing up in Paris," Buffet says, "my parents encouraged me to read and I spent a lot of time at the library. My favorite stories were myths and legends. It's impossible to recall all the books from those childhood years but I do remember the ones with good pictures. I looked at them over and over again."

Sometimes, if he liked a story that wasn't illustrated, Buffet did the drawing himself. He continued to develop his love for visual narrative in art school and kept dreaming that one day he'd get a chance to put together books of his own.

His opportunity finally came during the early 1970s when Buffet was asked by a Hawaii publishing company, Island Heritage, to do watercolor illustrations for a series of children's books based on local folktales. The first of these, *Kama Pua'a*, came out in 1972. Several more followed, including *Pua Pua Lena Lena* (1972), *Kahala* (1973), and *Makaha* (1974). All remain in print to delight today's youngsters.

This watercolor, "Christmas Eve at the Menehunes" is a recent work but it has obvious links to Buffet's classic folktale books. The menehunes, are the mythical little people of Hawaii who live primarily on the Garden Island of Kauai. Like their leprechaun cousins in Ireland, they are clever, industrious, and fond of practical jokes.

"Soon after one of those earlier books came out," Buffet says, "an old Hawaiian man came up to me and said he enjoyed it but that it wasn't the true legend. Maybe so, I answered, but what is a true legend anyway? I believe that a legend, like all art, is only limited by your imagination."

Private Collection

KAANAPALI

Kaanapali, on the sunny west coast of Maui, was a favored playground of the ancient Hawaiians. Its beautiful beach, clear waters, and cool tradewinds lured the royal families away from the stuffy capital of Lahaina during the hot summer months.

They erected temporary thatched shelters at Kaanapali and enjoyed the natural environment. During the day they fished and paddled their canoes in the ocean. At night, under the glow of burning torches, they held luaus and hula dancing.

After the Christian missionaries arrived in the 1880s most of the fun and games came to an end. The land was turned over to the farmers and sugar cane waved in these same tradewinds for the next century.

In the early 1950s, Amfac began looking at Kaanapali with the intention of developing it into a planned resort area. The first phase of the complex opened in 1962 and today it contains a dozen hotels and condominiums, two championship golf courses, and a shopping center built around its own whaling history museum.

Buffet, who lives a few miles away in Kapalua, has always found humor in the crowds of tourists who come to Kaanapali each year looking for their own idea of paradise. Some stay for weeks or months on end, never leaving their luxurious hotel rooms, fancy restaurants, and manicured beaches.

In this painting Buffet has isolated one of the most attractive corners of Kaanapali. He

has, however, exaggerated the famous West Maui Mountains. They are neither this steep nor this close to the ocean.

The building with the pyramid side is the Sheraton-Maui luxury hotel. It has won several architectural design awards. Next door to the hotel, Buffet has added a few private cottages to the grounds.

The cliff at the left is Black Rock, a sacred spot where ancient Hawaiians believed the souls of the dead leaped into the afterlife. An 18th century chief, Kahekili, won the respect of his men by jumping off here into the waters below. The practice later became proof of a young warrior's bravery.

Collection: Jack Dymond

COWS VISITING HUALALAI RANCH

Anyone familiar with Buffet's work knows that he paints a lot of cows. The painting opposite, "Cows Visiting Hualalai Ranch," and "Michel and his Tomatoes," on a previous page, are excellent examples. Buffet has painted hundreds of cows in recent years, many of them likely to appear in a future book of their own.

The best known is probably "Cows on Roller Skates," which was reproduced in the first volume of *Guy Buffet's Hawaii.* "That painting was done in 1979," he explains, "while I helped to raise my ex-wife's daughter, Nicole, between the ages of two and ten. During that time I would tell her all sorts of stories before she went to sleep.

"Once I made up a bedtime story about some cows who travelled home on roller skates. After hearing it, Nicole asked 'why don't you make a painting of that? It would be neat.' A few days later I did that painting for her and Nicole loved it. Everybody else seemed to like it as well."

Because of its popularity, "Cows on Roller Skates" was made into Buffet's first hand-pulled serigraph. There were 150 prints in the signed and numbered edition, priced at $250 each. Today it's hard to find one of these prints, even at $2,500.

This painting of Hualalai Ranch, located on the Big Island's Kona Coast, was commissioned by the owner. It is a large cattle ranch sprawling along the slopes of the inactive volcano from which it takes its name. On a visit to do some preliminary sketches Buffet stated that he'd never seen so many cows in one place.

"Hualalai Ranch also has a very beautiful setting," he says, "almost a paradise for cows. If cows could be tourists this is where they might want to go. The animals at the bottom of the painting are sightseers. Their cowboy tour guides have given them flower leis as a souvenir of the trip."

Collection: Mrs. Garner Anthony

SUGAR CANE DAYS

Sugar has played an important role in the history of Hawaii. No other single industry has created more jobs or generated more income for people in the Islands. It is often said that sugar built modern Hawaii.

"Most visitors think that sugar cane is native to Hawaii," Buffet says, "but actually it was introduced by the early Polynesian settlers. They brought sugar cane and other food plants along with them in their great voyaging canoes."

The Polynesians planted this sugar cane primarily as a hedge around their garden plots. If they got a desire for sweets they just broke off a stalk and chewed it for the juice.

When the Christian missionaries came to Hawaii in 1820 they knew that sugar could be made from the cane and traded for other products. The first successful sugar plantation in Hawaii was started by Ladd & Co. at Koloa, Kauai, in 1835. Their first 50-acre harvest was milled two years later, producing two tons of raw sugar that sold for $200.

In this painting Bufet has depicted the Pioneer Mill Company in Lahaina which began manufacturing sugar from cane in the 1860s. The mill, with its smokestack, is at left center while the homes of the workers are in the foreground along with the plantation's Chinese store.

By 1884 the Pioneer Mill Company had 600 acres under cultivation. The plantation also had its own railroad with a steam locomotive and 52 cars which were used to haul the cut cane in from the fields.

Pioneer Mill is still in operation today. Mechanization makes things easier but much of the labor is still done by hand. A restored version of the old train takes visitors for a ride through six miles of sugar cane and follows a section of the original track laid down a century ago.

*Collection: Southland Park
Montessori School*

ALOHA WEEK PARADE

Aloha Week is celebrated each fall in Honolulu and one of its highlights is a parade that winds its way through downtown Honolulu and into Waikiki. The lead rider in this painting is carrying the state flag of Hawaii. It was designed sometime before 1816 for Kamahameha I.

In the upper left corner of the Hawaii flag is a small British Union Jack. This was probably included to honor George Vancouver who presented the British flag to Kamehameha after the monarch placed his kingdom under the protection of Great Britain.

Beginning at the top, the flag has eight alternating white, red, and blue colors. These represent the eight major islands in the Hawaiian chain.

The parade is passing in front of the statue of Kamahameha I, located in front of the Aliiolani Hale, the Judiciary Building. This is the best-known sculpture in Hawaii and tourists frequently pose in front of it to get their photo taken.

In 1878 the kingdom commissioned Boston sculptor Thomas Gould to create a statue to honor Kamehameha I. Since no portraits existed of Kamehameha as a young warrior, Gould created his own likeness of the king. The idealized statue, of dark bronze and gilt, was modeled and cast in Florence, Italy. On its way to Honolulu, however, the ship sank and the statue was lost off the Falkland Islands in the South Atlantic.

"Fortunately," Buffet says, "the insurance money paid for a duplicate made from the first cast. The second casting arrived safely and was dedicated in 1883."

The lost statue was eventually recovered, repaired, and sent to the Kohala District of the Big Island, near Kamehameha's birthplace. In 1912 it was moved to its present location on the grounds of the Kohala Court House at Kapaau.

Private Collection

MAUI NO KA OI

This image is not an ordinary landscape. It is a dreamscape created entirely out of Buffet's fertile imagination. There is no such place on Maui, and never has been, but most viewers will immediately recognize it as a Valley Island scene.

Reproduced on the opposite page is a serigraph, or silkscreen stencil print, based on one of Buffet's original paintings. Forty-five screens were used to print this limited edition serigraph in 1981 by Accent Studios in Chatsworth, California.

Like many of Buffet's paintings and prints, this image was inspired on his many trips to the Hana Coast. "It is a composite of good times," he explains, "and dear friends. There aren't any bad memories in Hana."

Pictured at the bottom right is the famous Hasegawa General Store. This cluttered treasure chest of merchandise, run by Harry Hasagawa, is not only handy to residents but a popular stop for the town's sightseeing visitors. Harry's grandfather founded the store in 1910 and it's been a thriving family business ever since.

Bandleader Paul Weston celebrated the store in the 1970s when he wrote a catchy song entitled "At the Hasagawa General Store." Weston and his wife, singer Jo Stafford, often took their vacations in Hana.

In the center of this print is a yellow bus that belongs to Tiny Malaikini, a good-humored Hawaiian who is sitting behind the wheel. Tiny, who is anything but, leads tours around Hana. He was given his nickname by actress Susan Hayward who once visited Hana and asked for a bodyguard. She gave Malaikini the job because he was the biggest man in town.

Other familiar Hana sights in this print are the grazing cows of Hana Ranch, the secret valleys, the cliffside waterfalls, the historic 1838 Wananalua church, and a couple of the 56 one-lane bridges to be found along the twisting Hana Highway.

Standing on top of Tiny's tour bus is Buffet's favorite island band, Eddie Kamae and his Sons of Hawaii. "No Ka Oi" means "the very best" and for Buffet a party in Hana is about as good as it gets.

Collection: Mr. and Mrs. Moffett

A DAY UPCOUNTRY

The rolling hills of Upcountry Maui are sometimes called "The breadbasket of Hawaii." Its rich volcanic soil, cool mountain climate, and regular rainfall support a wide variety of agricultural properties.

"Upcountry is one of my favorite places in Maui," Buffet says. "Any time I'm in the area I stop to buy onions, lettuce, cabbage, peas, and other fresh vegetables."

During the 1840s and 1850s, local farmers raised Irish potatoes here and shipped them to the gold fields of California. It wasn't long before the Hawaiians were calling their land *Nu Kaleponi* (New California) because they were making more money than the gold prosecutors.

Today it is the onions, usually referred to as Kula Onions after the name of the district, that have become particularly well-known. Connoisseurs of such things say that Kula Onions are the sweetest in the world. Youngsters eat them raw like sugar cane.

Flowers are another major Upcountry product. The district grows most of Hawaii's carnations as well as the protea, an exotic plant originally from Africa that comes in an astonishing range of sizes and shapes.

"Protea blooms," Buffet says, "will last for weeks after picking and then get better with age. They dry into soft beautiful earth colors that will last for years."

Being a good Frenchman, Buffet also stops in regularly at Ulupalakua Ranch in the Upcountry. Here, on 20 fertile acres, the Tedeschi Vineyard and Winery produces a premium sparkling wine from its grapes.

The winery also bottles a popular sweet wine made from locally-grown pineapples. "My friends in Paris think I'm joking when I tell them we drink pineapple wine in Hawaii. I always bring along a couple of bottles when I go back for a visit."

Private Collection

PAU HANA

Despite the mild climate and casual lifestyle in Hawaii most islanders work as hard here as people do anywhere else. And, like everywhere else, when the job is done these hardworking fellows like to relax, grab a cold drink, and have fun with their buddies.

There are some obvious differences, however. When time clocks are punched out on the Mainland the workers often head for a favorite bar or to the nearest television set. In Hawaii, especially in more rural areas, they head for the beach, a community park or their neighbor's backyard.

"Pau Hana" is a local expression that means "through with work." This painting was commissioned by Gerald Sterns of Sterns & Ingram, a Honolulu law firm.

It was officially unveiled during a "through with work" party in 1985 at the Kahala Hilton.

"We had champagne and caviar at this party," Buffet says, "but most pau hana gatherings are fueled by a tub of cold beer on ice. For a snack you might find teriyaki chicken sticks, sushi, and sashimi or raw fish."

Music is also a big part of these get-togethers. There is always a guitar or ukulele around and everybody knows the words to the old Hawaiian songs. Stories and memories continue long after the sun goes down.

Buffet works hard at his art during the day and seldom turns down a pau hana party invitation from his friends. He often brings his sketch pad along to document the occasion.

When he has a pencil or pen in his hand everybody is on their best behavior. They know that they may eventually see themselves in one of his paintings.

"I do a lot of rough sketches of my friends," Buffet says, "and some of them are included in this book. When I need some new inspiration for a painting these sketches come in handy. If I still can't find what I want I just wait for pau hana time to roll by again."

Collection: Gerald Sterns

SKETCHBOOK

An artist keeps a sketchbook for many reasons. Quite often it's used as a kind of visual journal or diary, a means to record daily events, family, friends and new surroundings. At other times their sketchbooks provide places to work out the raw ideas that will eventually show up later in finished works of art.

The recently published sketchbooks of Picasso have thrown new light on this creative process. By the time of his death in 1973, at the age of 91, he had filled at least 175 known sketchbooks, containing over 7,000 drawings, and watercolors.

Guy Buffet, like Picasso, usually keeps a sketchbook close at hand. He uses it like some photographers use a camera: to document the people, places, and events that he wishes to experience, possess, and somehow filter through his unique imagination. Buffet's sharp sense of humor, of course, is evident in almost all of his sketchbook entries. Some of these informal pen-and-ink illustrations will inspire future paintings while others are complete in themselves. They may show up later on limited edition prints, posters, note cards, and books.

In the first volume of *Guy Buffet's Hawaii*, many of the artist's preliminary drawings were reproduced opposite to the related full-color paintings. They usually added an additional comment or insight to the work.

When it came time to put together *Fair Nights and Sunny Days*, Buffet decided on a different approach. The following pages feature a separate sketchbook that includes light-hearted illustrations of friends, various island "characters," and even a few of his famous Hawaiian cows.

The spirit of Amooha? Even that other sketchbook artist, Picasso, might have been amused.

Jimmy Buffett's Hawaii

Sketch Book

Lahaina Gallery Maui: the artist with two overbearing fans Jim Killett and Virgil Becker

Andrea Smith
for Love and Peace

Artists from Maui

[signature] ©87

Robert Lyn Nelson doing some research

CALYPSO

Parker Ranch: Going out?

AMO.O.O.O.HA!

On the beach: Mauna Kea

H.P.D "Take my heart"

Kapialani Park: the great pleasure of early morning Jogging © 1987

"Andy" of
Hasegawa General Store
Hana Maui

© 81

Harry Hasegawa Hana Maui

© 1987

What yu mean? yu da Boss???

Maui:
In the fields

Honolulu Lawyer

Honolulu ; downtown
Chinatown
Where the price counts not the style

Waikiki

Dear Erma.

Jam in paradise.....

Jimmy Buffett
© 1987

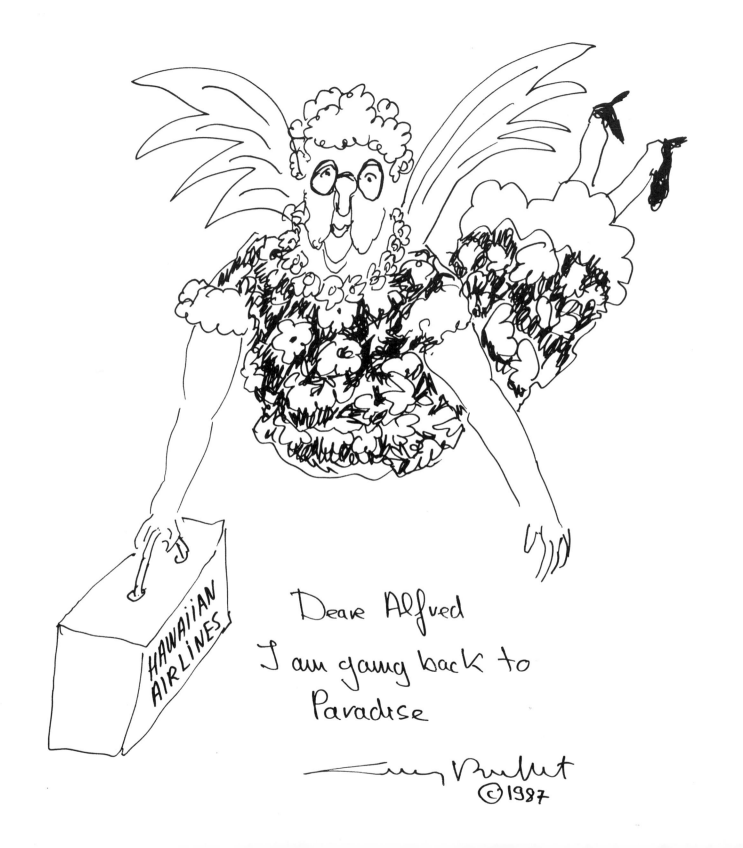

Dear Alfred
I am going back to
Paradise

Kauai Election Day

this is not
a toupée

Carl Lundquist
G.M. Hotel Hana Maui
© 1987

Mdokai
Felicio Pasquale
and his team
of champions
© 87

Young cow listening to her Walkman
on the slopes of Haleakala

Jim Mullet ©86

Kailua Kona.
Pig going to a Luau

Hey! tita.
Ono Shirley temple

Studies of titas,
tutus and......
da kine

© 1987

Lucien Charbonnier chef "Chez Paul" restaurant

Lahaina, Maui   [signature] ©87

Gerard Reversade and French kitchen veteran

Honolulu.
Law firm of
O.Connor, OLIVER
Carlsmith & SHKLOV

Aloha dear
old Conrad

© 1987

Downtown Honolulu, secretary day

MACADEMIA NUTS   OKOLEA

FOR CONGRESS
"PAT" ASAHI

Kaneohé, Oahu
Election day

Honolulu: Michel Martin with : tomato, chickeddy and sweet patouti *Guy Buffet* © 87

Waimanalo
Little kid going to
school
Guy Buffet
© 87

Picture! Please!!!
© 1987

Hawaiian Bankers © 87

Sometimes a great sadness
shows in the eyes of old "tutus"
Perhaps the memories of old Hawaii
blowored away for ever by the
winds of time......

_____ mullet ©87

On the courts: Kapalua
"Come on, Mac Enroe, let's give hem hell !!!!
©87

On the courts: Wailea.
a good volley

© 1987

Downtown Honolulu, Mauna Kea Street

Maui; Ulupalakua Ranch.   "I have nothing to wear"   Guy Buffet © 87

Member of the Outrigger Canoe Club Honolulu ©87

on the beach: Kaanapali

Kaanapali : meeting a friendly humuhunununkunukuapuaa !!!

Bob Longhi's home. Lahaina Maui : Two prawns making love under the influence of Amaretto.
© 1987

what the f...

Longhi's

Bob Longhi and his friend Freddy
© 87

fair nights and sunny days

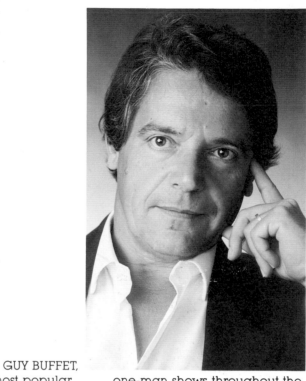

RONN RONCK, a well-known Hawaii journalist, is the travel editor and arts columnist for the *Honolulu Advertiser*. He was born in 1946 in Tulsa, Oklahoma, and graduated from the University of Tulsa in 1968. Ronck served with the U.S. Navy in San Diego and Guam, and later worked as a staff writer with Guam's *Pacific Daily News*. He moved to Hawaii in 1978 to work for the *Advertiser*. Ronck is the compiler and editor of *Ronck's Hawaii Almanac*, published by the University of Hawaii Press, and a contributing editor for *Hawaii*, a guidebook in the Apa Insight Guides series. In addition he has written the text for several photographic books for Mutual Publishing; including *Hawaiian Yesterdays: Historical Photographs by Ray Jerome Baker*, *Panorama Hawaii: Scenic Views of the Hawaiian Islands*, *Celebration: A Portrait of Hawaii Through the Songs of the Brothers Cazimero*, and *Kauai: A Many Splendored Island*. Ronck also edited the first volume of *Guy Buffet's Hawaii*.

GUY BUFFET, one of Hawaii's most popular artists, was born in Paris in 1943. He began to paint as a child and was enrolled at the age of 14 in the Beaux Arts de Toulon. From there he want on to study advanced art and design at the Academie de Peinture de la Ville de Paris. When he was 19 he joined the French Navy and sailed around-the-world as an official military artist. Buffet first visited Honolulu in 1963 and, a year later, returned to Hawaii after his military discharge. Since then he has had numerous one-man shows throughout the world and has authored and illustrated several folktale books for children published by Island Heritage. His original paintings and prints are highly sought after by collectors. The first volume of *Guy Buffet's Hawaii* was published by Cameron and Company in 1980. Cameron also publishes an annual wall calendar featuring his paintings. Buffet and his wife, Laurence, live in Kapalua, on the island of Maui, and in Paris.

Thank you very Much !!!

Gary Brullet ©87